K. Lee Roberts

# For the Love of God, Vote!

*A Christian's Guide*

Copyright © K. Lee Roberts, 2020
Published by CRA Press

ISBN 979-8660044496





To contact the author, please visit www.KLeeRoberts.com.

**My sincerest gratitude to the following individuals for their editing skills and treasured wisdom…**

Cindy Catuogno

Warren Caulton

Lynne LaBelle

Tina Metayer

Kim Morris

Cindy Rowley

Anne St. Denis

## A Note from the Author

*"For the Word of God is full of living power. It is sharper than the sharpest knife, cutting deep into our innermost thoughts and desires. It exposes us for what we really are."* (Hebrews 4:12)

Indeed! When writing this book and searching the Scriptures, I was reminded that before looking at candidates who are running for office, I should first examine myself with the very same questions being posed. Such an uncomfortable position in which to find myself! I wish you the same challenge as you read this. While voting is a method for expressing our beliefs, how much better would it be that each of us becomes a more faithful follower of Christ?

**Before You Begin**

We are tasked with asking ourselves the right questions, looking for godly characteristics, and voting with the conviction of what we know to be in line with the character of God. The attributes in the following pages have been gathered from both the Old and New Testaments. The Psalms, Proverbs, the life and teachings of Christ as found in the Gospels, and the letters to the early church are cited with the greatest frequency.

The Bible's teaching is relevant. It shows us what to look for in a leader and what to avoid. Whether you are a grade school student or biblical scholar, the principles are real and definable. The terms are straightforward. Simple concepts can be applied to complicated governance. Character has always mattered to God and it should matter to us.

While only God sees the hearts of people, we have to depend on a person's words and deeds as we prepare to cast our vote for them. Certainly we know that no one on earth today is perfect. As you compare candidates, their promises and their past actions, it is crucial to consider which individual embodies the traits of the only one who was sinless, Jesus, the Son of God. When presented with two or more individuals, ask which one is strongest in their words and actions. I hope the questions that follow will help in that endeavor. Whether you are casting your ballot in a local school committee race or in the presidential election, your vote matters.

I have sought characteristics and the ensuing questions to be those that are mentioned multiple times in God's Word. For instance, the Bible mentions love hundreds of times. Our love for God and each other is emphasized by Jesus and in the many letters of the New Testament. God has encouraged us to be good stewards of what He has provided; speaking to His creation, His gifts, and His truth.

# Good Judgment

How has the candidate sought out knowledge and insight in the past in order to make good choices?

When have you seen the candidate listening carefully to those charged with providing insight and information?

Do the decisions of the candidate reflect knowledge and wisdom?

# Compassionate

*Jesus showed His compassion for individuals and groups by taking action. He spoke to, healed, fed, and taught those around Him. (Mark 6:34, Matthew 14:14-21)*

Think of times you may have seen the candidate witness suffering or loss of life, whether due to natural disaster, illness, or injustice. How have you seen the candidate demonstrate compassion to those who are hurting?

Have you found their words to be comforting?

Does the candidate seem distressed by the pain and anguish of others?

# Protector of
# Children

How does the candidate protect the safety and well-being of children through their actions?

What evidence have you seen that indicates that the candidate values the lives of children?

What has the candidate done to invest resources to the education of all children?

How does the candidate encourage young people in their aspirations through engagement and by example?

# Patient

*Like many of the characteristics in this book, patience is*
*mentioned in the same sentence when describing love.*
*"Love is patient and kind. Love is not jealous or boastful*
*or rude. Love does not demand its own way."*
*(1 Corinthians 13:4,5a)*

How has the candidate shown patience when
dealing with others?

Does their demeanor change with the status or
position of the individual they are speaking with?

When answering questions, is the candidate
courteous and clear without condescension?

# Honest

*Jesus describes Satan in John 8:44, "[he] has always
hated the truth. There is no truth in him. When he lies, he
is consistent with his character."*

When you think of the candidate, do the words
honest and trustworthy come to mind?

What examples can you cite?

How does the candidate rate in the following:
Tells the truth, promotes the truth, and defends
those who tell the truth?

# Committed

*Esther was fully committed to do whatever was necessary to ensure the safety of her people even when the cost could have been her life. (Esther 4:14-16)*

What examples can you give of the candidate acting in the best interests of the people they serve?

What sacrifices has the candidate made in their career/time of service?

How does the candidate inspire others to be committed, resulting in a unified team working for the same cause?

# Cooperative

When have you seen the candidate work effectively with those who have differing viewpoints?

How has the candidate's cooperation helped or lack of cooperation hindered important goals being accomplished?

# Values Good Counsel

*We are reminded multiple times in the Bible to value good counsel. It is crucial to choose qualified, wise individuals to provide insight and keep us in check when we may tend to go astray. (Psalm 1:1, Proverbs 24:6)*

Who does the candidate look to for advice and insight?

When you look at the candidate's inner circle, do those individuals represent those whom they serve?

How does the candidate respond to disapproval by valued counsel?

# Recognizes the Power of Words

*The Bible has a lot to say about the words we use. In Matthew 12:35, Jesus says, "a good person produces good words from a good heart, and an evil person produces evil words from an evil heart."*

Do the candidate's words ultimately promote God's love and the values that Christ exhibited while on earth?




As a Christian, are you comfortable repeating the candidate's words?

# Diligent

What are some similarities of the candidate to the woman in Proverbs?

How has the candidate shown their vision and their willingness to work towards that end?

# Forgiving

When the candidate has been wronged by others, do they show a spirit of forgiveness?

What examples can you provide?

Does a lack of forgiveness interfere with the candidate's ability to do the job?

# Avoids
# Hypocrisy

Is there a significant gap between what the
candidate's words and their actions?

Have you observed the candidate criticizing their
opponents, but at the same time being guilty of
the same short-comings?

How does the candidate's treatment of others
reflect God's command to "love your neighbor?"

# Values Creation

*In Genesis 1, we see the record of God creating the world and all life within it. When He was done, He looked over all He had created and saw that it was "excellent in every way."*

How does the candidate communicate their awareness and respect that all people are created in God's image?

Science is the exploration of the intricacies of God's creation. List tangible ways that the candidate has used current scientific knowledge to support policies that protect His creation and the people He loves?

# Discerning

What are some examples the candidate may have demonstrated the ability to discern between sheep and wolves?

Is the candidate steadfast in their judgment, using the wisdom found in the Word of God as a gauge?

# Consistent

*In Psalm 119:5, the writer declares, "Oh, that my actions would consistently reflect Your principles!"*

Does the candidate act in a manner that is consistent with their proclaimed values?

Look at the candidate's past and proposed policies. Do you believe that God would approve of them?

# A Good Example

How has the candidate been a good example in
their lifetime?

Would you want your children to emulate the
words and actions of the candidate?

If you were to act like the candidate in your place
of work, would your co-workers be able to
recognize Christ in you?

# Faithful

*When telling the parable of the talents in Matthew 25:14-30, Jesus praises those who have been faithful in handling a small amount and gives them more responsibility.*

Given the candidate's handling of their past responsibilities, do they deserve to be put in charge of more?

How has the candidate exhibited faithfulness in the fulfillment of their personal and professional promises?

# Generous

When has the candidate been generous to others?

Does the candidate encourage others to help "the least of these?"

While financial giving is easy to quantify, how has the candidate given of their time, resources, and talents?

# Values a Variety
# of People

*Jesus went against societal norms when He talked with the Samaritan woman, ate with tax collectors, and healed lepers. Jesus was the human embodiment of God and we should seek to be more like Him. (John 4:9; Luke 15:1-2)*

Does the candidate speak with a variety of people?

How does the candidate affirm the value of all people, regardless of their financial or social status?

When the candidate speaks of other communities and countries, is respect for their people shown?

Look at the hiring practices of the candidate. Does the individual only hire people similar to themselves?

# Genuine

*We are told to genuinely love others, not just pretend. We are to "take delight in honoring each other." (Romans 12:9-10)*

Does the candidate delight in honoring others?

Are they people who act in a godly fashion?

Does the candidate's opinion of individuals vacillate from one day to another?

What does that say about the candidate?

# Loves God

Does the candidate acknowledge God in their life story?

While listening to a candidate's words, focus on their actions, past and present. What have their policies revealed about them?

# Good

*In Romans 12:21, we read, "Don't let evil get the best of you, but conquer evil by doing good." In Matthew 7:17-20, we're told that we can evaluate a person by the fruit that they produce.*

How has the candidate produced good fruit?

Can you imagine Jesus smiling at the work the candidate has done?

What worthy accomplishments can the candidate rightly claim?

# Grateful

*The Psalms are filled with verses encouraging us to be grateful to the Lord. In 1 Thessalonians 5:18, we are told, "No matter what happens, always be thankful."*

It's challenging to show appreciation during difficult times. How have you seen the candidate do this?

How is gratefulness reflected in the speech of the candidate setting the tone for their colleagues and constituents?

# Courageous

*We can see multiple places in the Bible where it says to be "strong and courageous." Any leader will have moments of trepidation when new and daunting situations arise. They will be required to go beyond that fear and move forward for the sake of those they serve. (Joshua 1:9, 1Corinthians 16:13)*

What examples of courage you have seen in the candidate's personal and professional life?

What difficult truths has the candidate spoken of and stood by?

When you close your eyes and imagine the candidate, do the words strong and courageous come to mind?

# Humble

*"Though He was God, He did not demand and cling to His rights as God." We are told to have the same attitude as Jesus. (Philippians 2:5-6)*

When you see the candidate, do they exemplify a person ready to serve regardless of the potential personal cost?

It's a challenge to have the confidence to say, "Vote for me," and at the same time be humble in their words. How does the candidate handle this?

# A Person of
# Integrity

*While the Lord does not define having wealth as a sin, He does condemn dishonest and dishonorable methods to gain money and power. (Proverbs 11:1-3)*

How has the candidate earned and managed their money? Are they transparent in their dealings?

Does the candidate enjoy considerable comfort while those who work for them are in poverty?

# Gentle

It can require strength and self-control to
respond with gentleness. When have you seen the
candidate act in a gentle manner?




Harsh words and actions are the opposite of
gentleness. Which is the candidate most likely to
exhibit?

# Encouraging

What encouraging words have you heard the candidate speak to lift up listeners in difficult times?

An effective leader inspires those on staff to be the best they can be for the benefit of all. How does their campaign and campaign staff reflect this?

# Just

*According to Micah 6:8, God requires us to "love justice." In 1 Corinthians 13:6, we are told that, "[love] is never glad about injustice but rejoices whenever the truth wins out."*

What are examples of the candidate seeking out justice for all people in their jurisdiction?



Does the candidate recognize injustice? How do they seek to be a part of the solution?

# Kind

*It's natural to be kind to your friends and people who agree with you. Jesus said in Matthew 5:43-48, that even the pagans do that. Being kind to those who are difficult requires intentional effort.*

How does the candidate respond when they are questioned?

Is the candidate consistently kind to all people, not just those who serve their purposes?

# Practices
# Humility

*Jesus said in Matthew 20:28, "I, the Son of Man, came here not to be served, but to serve others." He modeled this by washing the disciples' feet in John 13:1-17.*

What have you seen or learned about the candidate that would make you conclude that they have a servant's heart?

Does the candidate show a deference to people by not interrupting, letting them go first, and treating them with respect?

What acts of service have you seen in the candidate? (You often see them occur when they think no one is watching.)

Does the candidate seek to be a help when presented with the opportunity?

# Thinks on Good Things

*Proverbs 4:23 says, "Above all else, guard your heart, for it affects everything you do." According to Philippians 4:8, we are to "fix our thoughts on what is true and honorable and right."*

What sources of information does the candidate regularly consume?

How do the candidate's words correspond to thinking on honorable things?

# Values the
# Service of Others

How does the candidate show they value the hard work and service of others?

How do the candidate's policies and actions demonstrate respect for and support of those who have sacrificially served their country?

# Glorifies God

As you have observed the candidate over time, have they become more like Jesus? In what specific ways?

Look at the most recent speech given by the candidate. Can you envision the Lord using the same tone and words?

# Joyful

*Joy is mentioned as a fruit of the Spirit. We are told in the Bible many times to rejoice in the Lord. Jesus said our joy should overflow. (John 15:11, 17:13, Galatians 5:22-23, Philippians 4:4)*

When have you seen joy in the candidate? How was it expressed?

Do the words love and joy come to mind when you see the candidate?

# Peacemaker

How does the candidate exhibit a peace-loving heart through their actions and words?

What words does the candidate use to preserve peace when strife is running high?

How are the candidate's policies used to discourage violence?

# A Good Shepherd

*Jesus says that the good shepherd "lays down his life for the sheep." He has genuine concern for the sheep. (John 10:1-18)*

In difficult situations, how has the candidate protected the people they serve?


Has the candidate been willing to make personal and professional sacrifices in their leadership role?

# Responsible

How does the candidate demonstrate a sense of accountability to the citizens they work for?

How has the candidate responded to those in authority?

Does the candidate accept responsibility or assign blame when things go wrong?

When have you heard the candidate admit they were incorrect and attempt to make amends?

# Self-Control

*When reading through the book of Proverbs, the difference between the fool and the wise person is the characteristic of self-control. Peter shares that it is central to growing in Christ along with the attributes of patient endurance and godliness. (2 Peter 1:6-10)*

When you observe the candidate in their behavior, do they exhibit self-control?

How is self-discipline key in the leadership position the candidate is aspiring to hold?

Observing the candidate, how do they also embody the other characteristics of patient endurance and godliness in the above verses?

# A Good Steward

*God commands us to use what He has provided
responsibly and for His kingdom. This applies to all
aspects of our lives; financial, spiritual gifts, time, talent,
and power. We are called to be faithful stewards. (Luke
16:10-11, Colossians 3:23, 1 Peter 4:10)*

How has the candidate used all they have to
make life better for others?

What examples can you provide in the categories
provided above?

Has the candidate ever used their public office
for personal gain?

# Thoughtful

*In the book of James we hear, "My dear brothers and sisters, be quick to listen, slow to speak, and slow to become angry." (James 1:19)*

Does the candidate listen to others respectfully?

Would you say the candidate pauses to think before speaking?

Do their words show a quickness to anger?

# Vigilant

How does the candidate display their constant
diligence in managing the multiple facets of
complex issues?

What checks and balances are in place in the
candidate's life to get them back on track if they
start to veer off course?

# Behaves Like Jesus

*When Jesus was asked about the greatest commandment, He replied, "You must love the Lord your God with all your heart, all your soul, and all your mind. This is the first and greatest commandment. A second is equally important: 'Love your neighbor as yourself.' All the other commandments and all the demands of the prophets are based on these two commandments." (Matthew 22:37-40)*

Imagine Jesus as a candidate, how would He act?

What would He do in the job the candidate is seeking?

How does that compare with the behavior you see in the candidate?

# Now It's Your Turn

What other attributes do you think are important for a candidate to exhibit?

How can you support your answers using the Bible?

___________________________

___________________________

___________________________

___________________________

___________________________

___________________________

___________________________

___________________________

___________________________

___________________________

___________________________

___________________________

___________________________

___________________________

# <u>NOTES</u>

# <u>NOTES</u>

# NOTES

# NOTES

# NOTES

# NOTES

# NOTES

# NOTES

# NOTES

# NOTES

# Finally…

Thank you for taking the time to read this book. As Christians, we are charged to "pray without ceasing." Please continue to pray for wisdom and grace throughout the entirc election process.


For more from K. Lee Roberts, please visit www.kleeroberts.com.